In Bad We Trust

The Bad Kitty's Guide to Life

Katherine Blanc

Sourcebooks Hysteria™
An Imprint of Sourcebooks, Inc.®
Naperville, Illinois

Published by Sourcebooks, Inc.
P.O. Box 4410, Naperville, Illinois 60567-4410
(630) 961-3900
FAX: (630) 961-2168
www.sourcebooks.com

ISBN 1-4022-0499-X

Printed and bound in China
SNP 10 9 8 7 6 5 4 3 2 1

Dedicated with love to my mother,
Kathryn Banasky Boranian.

Bad Kitty

Attention All Kitties:

- Are you getting what you want from life?
- Are you feeling powerless in your human home?
- Are you wishing you were having more fun?
- Are you getting the attention you crave?

Now...

The Bad Kitty's Guide to Life has the answers.

The Bad Kitty way helps you deal effectively with humans and get more out of life. Demonstrations and time-tested tips put you back in control of your world without jeopardizing the many benefits of domestication.

Don't let opportunity pass you by!
Read **The Bad Kitty's Guide to Life**

When you follow the way of the Bad Kitty,
you can be sweet and sassy
at the same time.

A Bad Kitty is skilled in the art of being adorable.

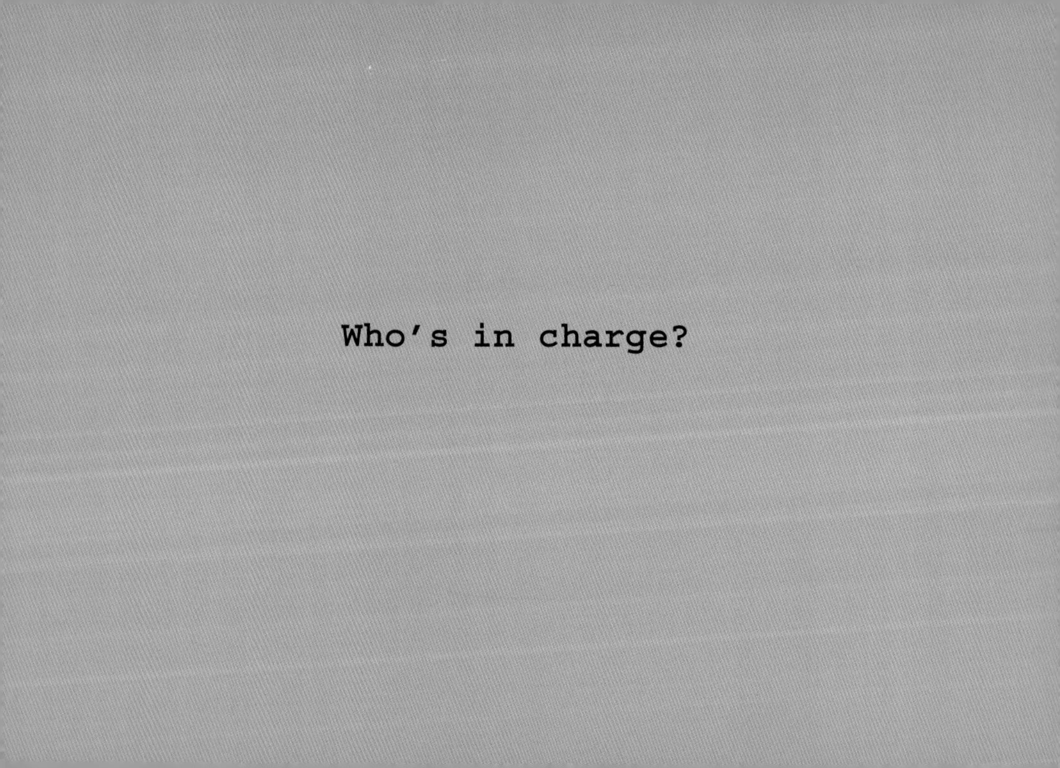
Who’s in charge?

Never arrive without a gift.

Eliminate the competition.

Human says:

"Here kitty-kitty"......................

"Get down!"............................

"Dinner's ready"......................

"Let me pet you"......................

"What a good kitty"..................

"I brought you a treat"..............

Kitty hears:

...........................“Watch out!”

...........................“Get cozy”

...............“Dinner’s on the table”

.....................“Let me brush you”

..................“Kitty’s in trouble”

..............“We’re going to the vet”

Some practices are
simply unacceptable.

Don’t let ’em
mess with perfection.

Any time, any place.

Leave a lasting impression.

KITTY
AT
WORK

KITTY
AT
PLAY

Rule with dignity.

Be productive.

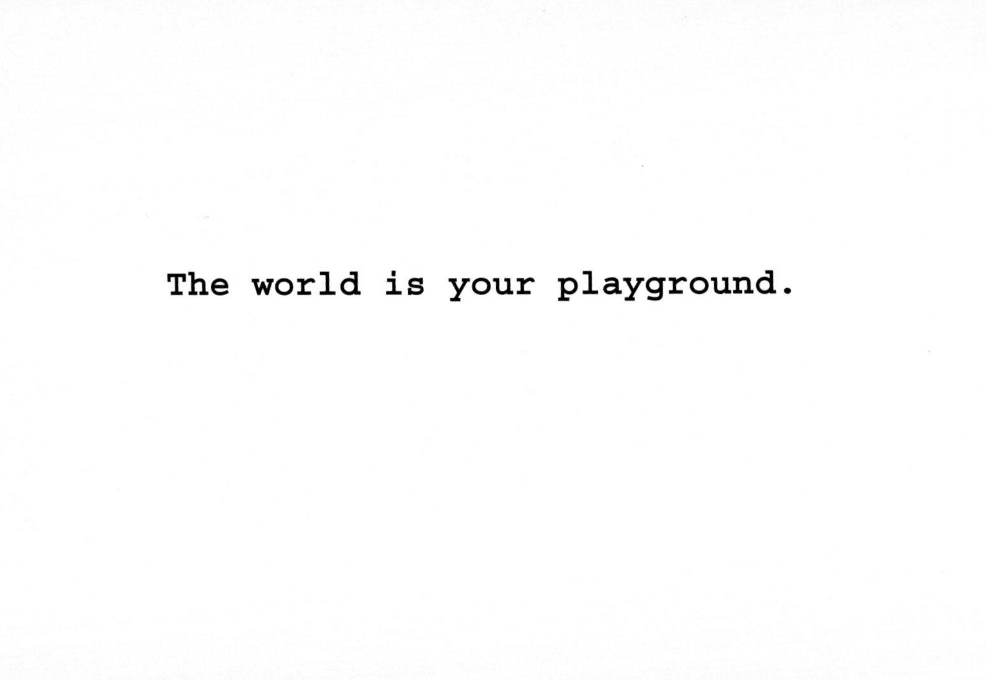
The world is your playground.

A kitty's gotta do
what a kitty's gotta do.

Retreat, but do not surrender.

Creative uses for
cheap cat food.

Buck
A
Bag

Catch, but DO NOT release.

Maintain complete innocence
at all costs.

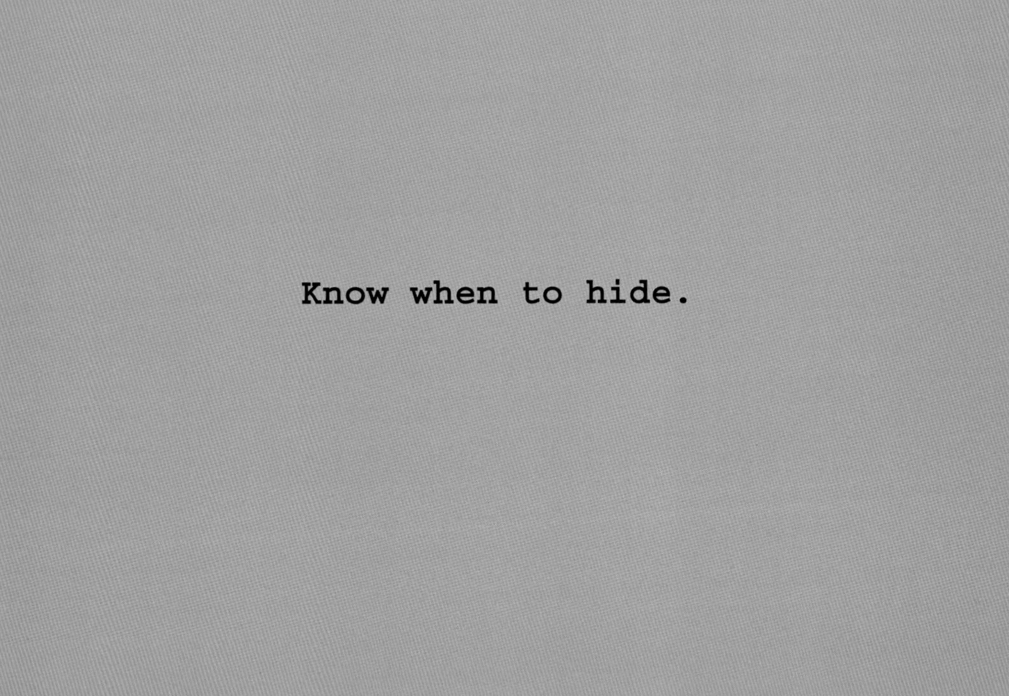
Know when to hide.

Claw your way to the top.

Stay on top of current events.

KITTY FANTASY

No. 1

Indulge yourself.

CATNIP
CATNIP

Get plenty of:

a.) Sleep
b.) Rest
c.) Naps

a.)

b.)

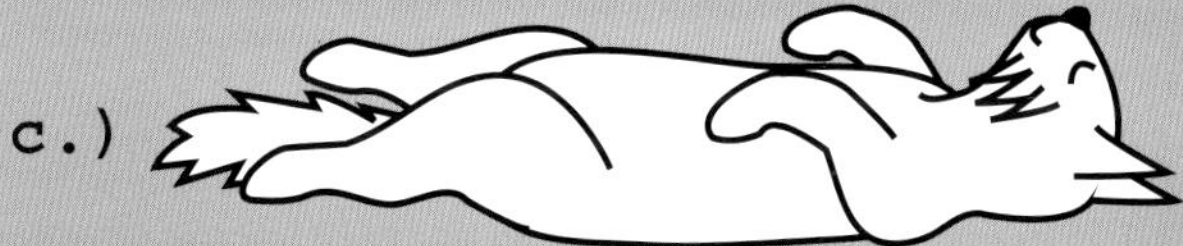
c.)

Discover the pleasures of gardening.

Kitty Fantasy #2

Enter
Exit

Establish your comfort zone.

It’s showtime!

In Bad
We Trust

In Bad
We Trust